Most taxonomists agree that the Red-eared Sliders belong to the genus *Trachemys*, but there are still many who argue in favor of their inclusion in either *Pseudemys* or *Chrysemys*. Photo by W. P. Mara.

PROFILE OF THE SLIDER TURTLES

The collective group of turtles known in common English as the "sliders" are currently placed in the genus *Trachemys*. *Trachemys* was first described by Agassiz in 1857, but the sliders have also been placed in synonymy with both *Pseudemys* and *Chrysemys* at one time or another until finally Seidel and Smith returned them to *Trachemys* in 1986, which is where they remain today. The argument over which of the three genera is most valid, or whether or not three separate genera are even necessary to begin with, seems quite complex and has posed a true state of taxonomic chaos to academics for many years.

There are six currently accepted species in the genus (Iverson, 1992), ranging from the "USA and Mexico, south to Argentina, [and the] West Indies." The only species occurring in North America is *Trachemys scripta*, which includes the Red-eared Slider, *T. s. elegans*, plus the Yellow-bellied Slider, *T. s. scripta*, the Big Bend Slider, *T. s. gaigeae*, and the Ornate Slider, *T. s. ornata*, among others. Sliders can be distinguished most easily by their rounded lower jaw (which is more "squared off" in *Pseudemys* species) and a patch of bright yellow or red on the sides of their heads.

Sliders are most often active during the daytime and can be seen basking in great numbers when the sun is out and the temperature has risen high enough. Like *Pseudemys* and *Chrysemys* turtles, sliders will not think twice before climbing atop other turtles if basking room is in short supply. They will also dive into the water without forethought if given proper cause, and the sight of a human definitely qualifies. Sliders can be found in a wide range of natural aquatic habitats including quiet ponds with heavy vegatation, muddy bottomed streams and rivers, and small woodland lakes thatched with fallen logs and decaying tree stumps.

GUIDO DINGERKUS

The turtle skeleton is truly fascinating. In this preserved specimen, the bones are in red and the cartilage is in blue.

The males of the genus do not generally grow as large as the females and will loose the bright juvenile coloration a little earlier on in life. The nails on their front claws are elongated (with the exception of those on the Big Bend Slider, *T. s. gaigeae*) and are used to caress the female's face during breeding. The young measure about 1 to 1 1/2 inches at birth and will grow to a maximum of about 11 inches in adulthood.

Sliders are mostly herbivorous, feeding on plants and so forth, but some have been known to take carrion in the wild and will accept some red meat in captivity.

SPECIES AND SUB-SPECIES

Included here for reference purposes is a general checklist of the species and subspecies of the genus *Trachemys*. All data is as current as possible (Iverson, 1992), and, to the best of the author's knowledge, wholly accurate and reliable.

Trachemys decorata (Barbour and Carr, 1940)
No currently accepted subspecies

Trachemys decussata (Gray, 1831)
d. decussata (Gray, 1831)
d. angusta (Barbour and Carr, 1940)

Trachemys dorbigni (Dumeril and Bibron, 1835)
d. dorbigni (Dumeril and Bibron, 1835)
d. brasiliensis (Freiberg, 1969)

Trachemys scripta (Schoepff, 1792)
s. scripta (Schoepff, 1792)
s. callirostris (Gray, 1855)
s. cataspila (Gunther, 1885)
s. chichiriviche (Pritchard and Trebbau, 1984)
s. elegans (Wied, 1839)
s. emolli (Legler, 1990)
s. gaigeae (Hartweg, 1939)
s. grayi (Bocourt, 1868)
s. hartwegi (Legler, 1990)
s. hiltoni (Carr, 1942)

There are 15 other subspecies in *Trachemys scripta* beyond the Red-eared Slider. Most of these subspecies never make their way into the turtle-keeping hobby. Shown here are five small *Trachemys scripta grayi*.

s. nebulosa (Van Denburgh, 1895)
s. ornata (Gray, 1831)
s. taylori (Legler, 1960)
s. troostii (Holbrook, 1836)
s. venusta (Gray, 1855)
s. yaquia (Legler and Webb, 1970)
Trachemys stejnegeri (Schmidt, 1928)

s. stejnegeri (Schmidt, 1928)
s. malonei (Barbour and Carr, 1938)
s. vicina (Barbour and Carr, 1940)
Trachemys terrapen (Bonnaterre, 1789)
No currently accepted subspecies

HOUSING

Once you acquire your new slider turtle, the first concern you should have is where to keep it. There are a number of fine points to be considered since chelonians can be quite delicate and somewhat demanding.

TYPES OF TANKS

Since sliders are dedicated swimmers, they will primarily need quarters which can comfortably contain a large water mass. Thus, building your own tank out of wood (which many hobbyists enjoy doing) is more or less out of the question unless you can make it large enough to include a separate container of water. But since that container would have to be constantly cleaned anyway, and seeing as how the turtles would not spend much of their time on land in the first place, it is ill-advised to use this approach at all.

Standard glass aquariums work best with *Trachemys* species. They can be acquired at any pet store, in a variety of shapes and sizes, and are relatively inexpensive.

One of the nicer aspects of glass tanks is that they can be cleaned thoroughly—a major consideration when housing aquatic turtles. Although filtration will help keep filth down, a tank that houses *Trachemys* turtles must be of the

The River Tank System RT30 combines a variety of elements into a complete ecosystem and can be used with any small slider turtle.

kind that a keeper can scrub to near sterility.

TANK SIZE

Relatively speaking, sliders grow to a fairly large size. An adult, for example, over 6 inches in carapace length is not at all unusal, so the size of your tank will depend directly on the size and number of sliders you intend to keep.

The best size tanks for most sliders are 20-, 30-, and 55-gallon aquariums, whichever one chosen will depend on size and number of specimens.

TANK TOPS

For any tank, there are a great number of tops available. Some have fine-mesh screening while others have quarter or eighth-inch hardware cloth, and yet others have a flip-top hood with a light built in. Any of these can be obtained at your local pet store, where they will either be in stock or can be ordered.

However, the most important characteristic a turtle tank top must have is the ability to allow direct rays of something called full-spectrum lighting, which is discussed in detail elsewhere in this book.

In many cases tops are not even necessary since most sliders will not be able to "escape" from a standard glass aquarium in the first place. Also, some keepers like to suspend their full-spectrum bulbs well over the tank's opening, in which case a top would then be detrimental to the sought effect. However, if a slider is kept in a room where cold drafts and breezes may be present, then a top is advised as a safety measure.

water that screams of visual esthetics. The problem lies in the fact that sliders need their water more than just *looking* clean; it must *be* clean. A keeper of any aquatic turtle must accept the fact that sliders are very messy creatures. Unlike a snake or a lizard, which may not soil a clean tank for a week or so, a slider placed in a sparkling tank will defecate

PHOTO COURTESY ROLF C. HAGEN CORP.

Advanced Aquarium Starter Kit. For the keeper of small slider turtles, it would be a good idea to set up your first tank using the basic starter kit shown here. You won't, of course, be filling the water up to the tank's rim.

FILTRATION

Often a beginning turtle hobbyist will ask about the effectiveness of filtration in conjunction with aquatic turtles like the sliders. It seems there are an enormous number of "filtration systems" used for this purpose: undergravel filters, box filters, "rim" filters, etc.

The problem is, assuming one uses a filter in order to cut down on water changes, a slider's tank water has to be disposed of and replaced whether you decide to use filtration or not.

A filter's job is to remove small particles of junk from the tank, to create an attractive, clean body of

within a day; sometimes an hour or so.

So whichever filtration method you choose, the water will still have to be dumped, the tank scrubbed, and then fresh water added. This can be laborious and time-consuming, but it's the practice of good husbandry and goes with the territory.

Corner box filters are probably the least expensive, but with that I have also found them to be the least effective. Even the smallest ones are about 3 inches high, meaning the water level has to be at least 4 or 5, and that kind of water mass is either too much for a tank like a 20-gallon

A resident of Brazil, Argentina, and Uruguay, the Brazilian Slider, *Trachemys dorbigni*, is a resident of slow-moving waters with soft bottoms, thick vegetation, and numerous basking sites. Photo by Harald Schultz.

or too broad for the filter to function in anyway.

A similar debate can be applied to "rim" filters; these attach to a tank's rim and have a long, broad tube that extends into the water, replacing the water by way of a "waterfall" of sorts. You can't attach these to much more than an ordinary aquarium, and even if you fill the tank high enough to where the filter will be functional, the sound of the water falling from that distance will slowly drive you, or at the very least your sliders, crazy.

Thus, by process of elimination, undergravel filters are probably best. They are not cheap, but for the purpose they are most efficient. Acquiring some of the better

accessories will allow you to run the tank virtually without a sound, and changing dirtied filters can be taken care of easily enough. Of course, with an undergravel filter you will

The Supreme Ovation Filters are a series of filters that are highly recommended for the keeper of aquatic turtles. They can be laid on their side and are quiet and very efficient.

PHOTO COUTESY E.G. DANNER MFG.

need a reasonably light substrate. A half-inch layer of ordinary aquarium stones, packed loosely, will do nicely. Packing them tightly will restrict the filter's overall performance.

LIGHTING

If there is but one thing captive Lizards and turtles have in common that other herptiles do not, it is a dependency on something called full-spectrum lighting.

In essence, full-spectrum lighting is a form of artificial illumination that

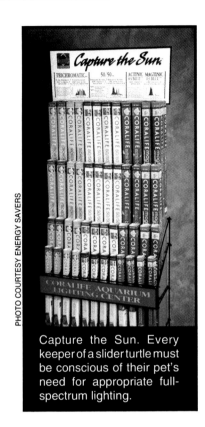

PHOTO COURTESY ENERGY SAVERS

Capture the Sun. Every keeper of a slider turtle must be conscious of their pet's need for appropriate full-spectrum lighting.

not only sustains a captive animal's day/night cycle, but also replicates and provides radiant energy given off in nature by the sun.

During the process, a collection of vitamins (mostly D3) are absorbed into the recipient's body through direct exposure to such light. This in turn encourages proper bone formation, among other things. In the wild, snakes, salamanders, frogs, toads, caecilians, etc., benefit from direct sunlight but do not need it in order to survive. Some lizards and turtles, however, will die within 8 months to a year if denied this.

Thus, the keeper of sliders is responsible for the reliable

provision of full-spectrum lighting. This can be done easily enough by taking a trip to your local pet store and purchasing any of several brands of fluorescent lights specially designed for use with reptiles. Some places may only stock, or at that particular moment only have in stock, something commonly called a "black light." Black lights emit a very dark purple beam and are often used in conjunction with horticulture.

But a number of tests done with black lights and turtles have shown that not only do turtles benefit less from black lights (in comparison to full-spectrum lights), but frequently a turtle's vision will be damaged due to the intense quality of the beam. Some subjects even suffered permanent blindness, and within a very short time.

A "catch" to full-spectrum lights that you may find irritating is the fact that they are somewhat expensive. Unfortunately I cannot say much more than this is simply the way it seems to be and there is not much to be done about it. However, there is no concrete rule that says you must buy

The Reptile Brightlight Heat Lamp provides purified full-spectrum daylight that simulates the natural photoenvironment of the reptile's habitat.

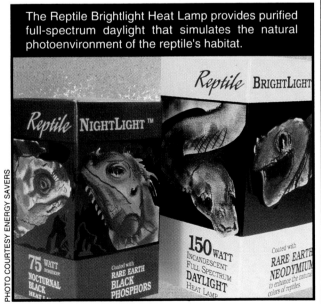

PHOTO COURTESY ENERGY SAVERS

one light for each and every tank you have. In fact, I used to move my light to a different tank every 3 days. I found the turtles still benefitted from the full-spectrum bulb even though it only came to them every week or so.

A second option, if you have a reasonably small number of tanks, is to simply suspend the bulb over two or more aquariums. A full-spectrum beam has to be very far away from a turtle in order for the effectiveness to wane. In a normal domestic household, most ceilings aren't quite that high anyway.

Along with the quality of the light goes the duration; something called *photoperiod*. In simple terms, photoperiod is how long a light stays on and off. In the wild this is represented by the time of year, i.e., the duration in which the sun shines each day, which is of course decided by the seasons. In a slider's natural habitat the sun will shine longer in the summer and shorter in the winter. Thus, the gradual increase or decrease of sunlight lets the slider know what time of year is approaching. This is most important at the beginning of spring and fall.

In the case of the former, when a slider knows breeding time is coming

it will begin to behave appropriately. Likewise, when the lengths of the days begin to gradually grow shorter, the animal will begin to prepare for hibernation during the winter months.

Since the keeper probably has better things to do with his or her time than become tied down to a turtle room twice a day to turn the lighting on and off, it is advised that a simple timer be bought. The unit can of course be adjusted to replicate whichever season is drawing near and lifts the burden of this tiny yet vital responsibility from the keeper's daily routine.

PHOTO COURTESY ROLF C. HAGEN CORP.

Marina Aqua-Decor. To add a touch of beauty to a slider's tank setup, you can always slip a little scenery onto the back wall of the tank.

HEATING

As with any other captive reptile, a *Trachemys* turtle should be kept warm at all times (during the active season of course). The average temperature should be around 75°F, as that is close enough to the temperature in their natural environment and will allow them to function normally.

Providing this is simple enough, but may be expensive. Not only does the water need warming, but the air as well. You should not, for example, leave a slider in a cold room and simply heat its pool area. What happens when the turtle wishes to

Four Paws Safety Screen Covers are designed to fit any size tank. The locking system ensures the pet's safety.

The natural area in which many slider turtles occur can be replicated to a respectable, although obviously miniaturized, degree in captivity. All you really need is a large tank and some aquatic plants.

spend some time on dry land?

Since they do spend most of their time in water, this is the area that needs to be warmed the most. This can be done easily enough by utilizing one of the many aquarium-heating products on the pet market. The easiest and most obvious is the fully submersible heater, which looks like a long glass tube with a coated wire protruding from one end. These

specimens. During feeding time, and occasionally during other times as well, a large slider may accidentally, or even intentionally, snap at the electrical cord and cut through the coating. There's no real need to point out what will happen next.

A second heating method is the under-tank heating pad. These have enjoyed a colossal degree of popularity in the herpetological

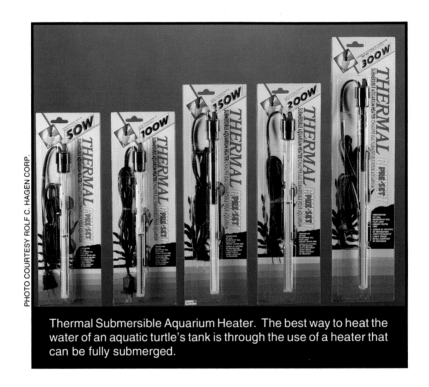

PHOTO COURTESY ROLF C. HAGEN CORP.

Thermal Submersible Aquarium Heater. The best way to heat the water of an aquatic turtle's tank is through the use of a heater that can be fully submerged.

are very nice because they have a built in thermostat and thus can be set to the perfect temperature. They were designed for the fishkeeping hobby but can obviously be used in any capacity the buyer wishes. They are not terribly expensive, and come in a variety of sizes and wattages. Since your slider tank will probably not boast an enormous water region, you will very likely get by with the smallest model. The only danger you should be made aware of is using this type of heater with large, aggressive

hobby over the last few years and are used in every facet of reptile and amphibian husbandry. If the tank you keep your sliders in has a water body that is in direct contact with the floor of the tank (as opposed to a water body that is kept in a separate container), a heater of this kind can be most useful. Beware, though, of those models that do not have a built in thermostat. It is important that the keeper has control of the water's temperature. Also, these may not be usable with plastic tubs, since extended contact could very well soften and even melt the plastic material.

Finally, if you have a large number of turtle tanks and do not feel it would be practical for you to heat each one separately, you can purchase a small external heater for the room itself. In this case, not only is the ambient air temperature maintained, but in most cases the water temperature is rendered safe as well. Perhaps it will not be as warm as the turtles may like it, but they are flexible in this respect and will survive nevertheless. Most room heaters today have built-in thermostats and are affordably priced. The type that is referred to as a "ceramic" heater is, I have found, much easier on the electric bill as well.

TANK CLEANING

Of course, a slider's tank is going to have to be cleaned frequently if you wish to assure a safe home for it. Even a good filtration system cannot replace the need for this practice. Thus, it is advisable for the keeper to design a competent routine and then a comfortable schedule for him- or herself, and stick to it responsibly.

I have been cleaning turtle tanks on a regular basis for many years, so I will share with you my own step-by-step method. You of course don't have to follow it to the letter, but it will make a dependable blueprint for your own situation.

PHOTO COURTESY ROLF C. HAGEN CORP.

Floating Thermometer. It is always a good idea to keep tabs on the water temperature of your slider's tank. Therefore, a floating thermometer is advised.

Assuming you have an oridnary glass aquarium, or at the very least a large plastic tub, refer to the following instructions:

1) Gather the proper equipment—an old towel, a sponge, a pair of containers—one in which to temporarily place the turtles and the other in which to place other tank items (rocks, filters, etc.)—if you have a fully submersible heater then you will need a small container filled with warm water to place it in, and if you have a reusable substrate then you will need a bucket to dump and clean it in, some liquid dish soap, and a small amount of bleach.

2) Remove the sliders and place them in their temporary holding quarters.

3) Remove all other tank implements, placing them in their own respective containers as well.

4) Dump the tank water. If you have a heavy substrate like rocks or stones, be careful not to tip the tank too quickly or you may cause the bedding to drop and crack the glass.

5) Dump out the substrate. Dispose of it if it is not re-usable, or place it in the bucket if it is.

6) Fill the tank about one-eighth of the way with warm, soapy water, and add in a small amount of bleach. Mix thoroughly.

7) Using the sponge, gently but firmly scrub all sections of the tank (outside as well if so desired) until you are satisified as to the overall cleanliness.

8) Dump the dirty water and rinse the tank thoroughly in cold water. It is crucially important that all residue from the bleach be removed, so you

and return the submersible heater if that is what you are using. Be careful not to refill the tank with cold water or the temperature shock may cause

All slider turtles need to have their tank regularly cleaned whether the water is filtered or not. Shown is the Central Antillean Slider, *Trachemys stejnegeri*.

may want to rinse more than once.

9) Dry the tank and replace it in its original resting spot.

10) Use the same soap/bleach mixture on the reusable substrate (if you are using one) and the tank implements. Again, rinse thoroughly. Replace all filter materials as well.

11) Fill the tank with clean water

the heater to crack.

12) Now, taking a separate sponge (one that has not been introduced to bleaches or soaps) gently "wash" each slider under a stream of lukewarm water. This helps clean away any mild fungal growths on the shell and is a good practice to get into.

13) Replace turtles. Done.

M. FREIBERG

Trachemys dorbigni brasiliensis. Small slider turtles are particularly susceptible to disease and therefore their tanks must be cleaned a little more often than those of the adults.

Many slider turtles can withstand fairly cool water temperatures, but those that occur in tropical or subtropical waters, like this Jamaican Slider, *Trachemys terrapen*, will need their water heated.

R. D. BARTLETT

Basking spots are crucial to the housing of slider turtles. Sliders are among the most devout baskers in the turtle community. Photo of the Red-eared Slider, *Trachemys scripta elegans*, by Michael Gilroy.

FEEDING

FOOD ITEMS

For any hobbyist who wishes to keep a slider, luck is on his or her side when it comes to food items. Not only are *Trachemys* turtles willing and eager feeders, but their diets vary highly as well. In the wild they are highly herbivorous, but in captivity they can be trained to take any number of things, which of course plays an enormously important role in keeping them healthy.

COMMERCIAL FOODS

For most keepers, the easiest way to feed a captive turtle is out of a can. There are quite a number of these products on the pet market at present, and most have, over the course of time, proven themselves to be reliable enough.

Nutra-Fin Turtle Pellets. For keepers who want to make feeding their turtles an easy chore.

The problem is, more often than not a slider that has recently been introduced to captivity will not respond to such foods but will instead need its appetite "jump started" by something a little more familiar to it.

For example, I once kept a beautiful adult male Yellow-bellied Slider, *Trachemys scripta scripta*, that I obtained from a commercial dealer on the upper East Coast. The animal was obviously wild-caught and seemed rather displeased because of it. I knew this could mean trouble, but nevertheless it looked very healthy and I found myself drawn to the challenge.

I took the animal home and left it alone in a moderately warm water tank for about 4 days. Then I changed the water and dropped in three sticks of a very popular commercial turtle food. I wasn't expecting him to attack the sticks with any great vigor, but was both surprised and disappointed when he didn't even acknowledge them at all.

I obviously had to try another approach since it seemed the "easy way out" would not be of any use to me. I consulted a reliable field guide to find out what the turtle ate in his natural habitat (leafy aquatic plants, some small insects, earthworms) and decided, in desperation, that I had to obtain one of these things in order to get *something* in the turtle's belly, even if it meant going to considerable trouble.

In the end I managed to obtain some nice, fat earthworms from a friend's backyard, and sure enough the turtle responded. Unfortunately, that was the only thing it would eat for the time being, and after about ten trips, my friend's backyard looked like a detonated minefield.

This went on for about two long, arduous months, and then the turtle finally started taking something else: crickets. That was certainly an improvement since they could be obtained easily enough at my local pet store. But still, giving him that commercial food was my true goal.

Every week I tried some—a few pieces along with the crickets—but with no results. So I ceased the addition of commercial sticks for about a month, and then the most wonderful things happened.

I gave the turtle its usual meal of half a dozen crickets (every fourth day) and then threw in two pieces of commercial food, and this time, he took them. Furthermore, he must have found the sticks much to his liking because less than 2 weeks later he went after the commercial food *first*, then took the crickets afterward.

The point of the story is, just because you have a slider that seems disinterested in commercial food today, that does not mean it won't feel differently tomorrow. Keep trying the "canned" stuff; you may find that one day the animal won't be able to get enough of it.

CRICKETS

As far as live foods go, crickets are probably offered to sliders more than any other item. Good thing, too. Crickets are an excellent meal for turtles. They are one of the few items a keeper can obtain without too

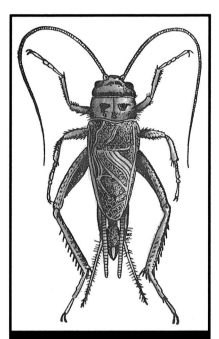

Crickets are perhaps the most common and easily obtained slider turtle food item. They are indeed a complete meal and can be given on a regular basis. You can even sprinkle them with vitamin powder the night before offering them.

much trouble that gives the turtle a completely nutritional meal.

Most pet stores that stock herpetological goods will sell crickets. Crickets are reasonably inexpensive and occasionally are offered in a variety of sizes.

If the pet store you frequent has trouble providing crickets on a regular basis, you can order them in bulk from a breeding farm. These places can be contacted through any one of a number of popular herpetolgical magazines, newsletters, or societies. The prices are almost always reasonable and delivery can usually be depended upon within a day or two.

Some keepers are fortunate enough to live in areas where crickets not only occur naturally but are even very abundant. If you are one of those people, you can capture crickets in quantity (during the warmer months of course) by placing a few pieces of black tarpaper in random spots where crickets are known to occur. After about 3 days, check under these pieces daily since the crickets will then be using them for shelter. Remember to be quick, because they certainly will. Grab one by placing your flattened palm over it as quickly yet as gently as possible, then close your hand and you

Strips of lean meat are usually taken with great eagerness by captive slider turtles, but be careful that you only offer this as a treat. Most meats are simply too fatty to be given regularly. Photo by Susan C. Miller.

should have it. Place them in a small tank with a secure top and give them plain oatmeal and a wet sponge for water, then simply draw from them as you need to.

EARTHWORMS

Another superb dietary item, and one that most emydid turtles (members of the family Emydidae, including sliders, cooters, box turtles,

MICHAEL GILROY

Earthworms and mealworms will certainly be accepted by slider turtles with great eagerness, and these two items are rarely a problem for the keeper to obtain, but they should be offered only in supplement and not as staple items because neither is nutritionally complete.

MICHAEL GILROY

One of the most appealing features of the slider turtles is their voracious appetite. With proper attention to providing a balanced diet, you can assure yourself of having beautiful specimens like the pair of Red-eared Sliders, *Trachemys scripta elegans*, shown here. Photo by Isabelle Francais.

etc.) eat with great enthusiasm in the wild, is the earthworm. Earthworms provide a nutritionally adequate, although not complete, meal for sliders and, like crickets, can often be found right in one's own backyard.

The trick here is to place a piece of moist linen or other similar fabric on the ground where the soil is very soft

Reptile Ten was specifically designed as a floating food stick for aquatic reptiles; like a number of other commercially prepared turtle foods, it contains added vitamins and minerals.

home. If you have to travel any great distance to obtain them and have no choice but to keep them domestically, then simply fill a tank with about 4 inches of potting soil and cover the soil surface with fresh leaf litter, replacing it every week or so. Be sure to keep the soil moist as well.

If you find yourself nowhere near a natural source of earthworms but would like to feed them to your *Trachemys* stock nevertheless, you can always try to locate a fisherman's bait store. Worms can be purchased in large quantities and either kept alive in the same fashion outlined above or frozen and then thawed as your needs dictate. If you decide to take the latter approach be sure to wrap and freeze each worm individually or they will stick together in one giant mass. Plus, don't forget to "stock up" on worms for the colder winter months since they not only will not be available in the wild, but are often unavailable commercially as well.

and fertile (compost piles are also acceptable). Make sure the fabric remains moist, and every couple of days simply peel it off the ground surface and harvest your worms. They can be given to the turtles immediately (although I would suggest washing off the residual soil first) rather than maintained in one's

MEALWORMS

Another item commonly seen for

Beetles are, unlike earthworms, a nutritionally complete meal for slider turtles, but be careful when offering them to young turtles because the beetles can be very vicious and may cause the turtles harm.

The beautiful Yellow-bellied Slider, *Trachemys scripta scripta*, does just as well in captivity as any of the other sliders and appears occasionally in the pet market. Photo by K. T. Nemuras.

W. P. MARA

Virtually all aquatic turtles will take their meals while in water, which will probably cause a lot of headaches for the keeper who values cleanliness. Perhaps an easily removable tub like the one shown here is the answer.

sale in pet stores is the mealworm. Mealworms are larval beetles and can be used as a dietary additive for many captive creatures besides slider turtles. Frogs, toads, lizards, salamanders, birds, fish, etc., all benefit from mealworms.

The problem is they are an incomplete item and at best should be offered as supplements. They do not provide sliders with the calcium they so desperately need for shell growth and so forth.

Mealworms can be obtained both in the pet stores and through the mail. Or, if you have a bit of extra space and think you can handle the odor, you might want to try breeding them yourself. This can be accomplished easily enough by first purchasing about 200 mealworms

and letting them transform into full-adult beetles. Place them in an opaque sweater box with about a 3-inch layer of oatmeal or bran. Keep the lid on tight (with one or two small ventilation holes) and just wait. Within a few weeks the mothers should begin laying eggs, which in turn will hatch, and a new generation will have begun. If you spare most of these first newborns for the purpose of beginning another colony, in time you will have a steady, unbroken stream.

RAW FISH/CARRION

Some sliders appreciate a little fish in their diet and will grab for it with great fervency. Fish can be obtained in both live and dead form, any place from a pet store to a supermarket.

Obviously dead fish will be easier for your sliders to grab hold of, but every now and then I like to give mine a little exercise by making it chase its food down rather than simply hand it over.

Try to avoid fish that are overtly salty as they are simply too unnatural for freshwater turtles. If you have acquired a portion that you feel is too salty, you can soak it in ordinary tap water for a while, alternately squeezing the "meat" and rinsing it out. This should remove not only much of the salt, but the oils as well.

Goldfish are an acceptable variety and are certainly inexpensive enough, and dead fishes can be bought at a fish market or supermarket seafood section. Again, most portions will be relatively inexpensive and are available all year. If the segment is too large and needs to be kept for a while, simply cut it up into "week long" sections (parcels that will remain fresh and usable at ordinary refrigerator temperature for one week) and freeze the rest, making sure each section is wrapped individually so it does not adhere to the other pieces. From here you can remove each piece when needed and defrost it in a bowl of warm water.

A final note concerning dead fish—another reason why hobbyists should avoid offering it too often is because it really wreaks havoc on the sanitary state of the tank water. No matter how long and how vigorously you drain a piece of raw fish, a greasy film will still appear on the water's surface

Trachemys scripta venusta (Meso-American Slider). Never assume there is something your slider turtle will not eat, because you never know. As long as the item in question is beneficial to the turtle's health, try it.

R. D. BARTLETT

and below it will become cloudy and filthy. It is a given that each time you offer raw fish to your sliders you will have to change the water no more than a day (at the longest) afterward. Even if you take each turtle out and feed it in a separate tank, enough oil

make in bulk and keep in a separate container in the refrigerator. Vegetables are wonderfully nutritious and can be offered any time.

MISCELLANEOUS LIVEFOODS

If you happen to own a slider that

DR. HERBERT R. AXELROD

Even though newborn sliders will very probably be hardy eaters with healthy appetites, chances are you will have to chop up whatever food items you plan to give them, if for no other reason than just so they can get the food in their mouths!

will adhere to its shell to infect the water in the regular tank.

VEGETABLES

Since sliders are basically herbivorous in the wild, they will greatly appreciate a few bits of vegetable matter at feeding time. Fortunately for the keeper, vegetables can be bought at any supermarket or roadside stand, or if it turns out your sliders like them enough, you might even want to start up your own crop in the backyard.

Carrots, lettuce, cabbage, beets, radishes, cucumbers, etc., can all be chopped up into tiny cubes and tossed into the tank. You may even want to formulate some sort of personal "recipe," which you can then

seems to enjoy livefoods and tends to be a bit more carnivorous than herbivorous, you should by all means endeavor to give it what it wants. Crickets and mealworms are not the only tiny creatures a hungry turtle will take. I have given my own specimens spiders, slugs, grasshoppers, and even large ants. There will very probably come a time in your turtle's life when the urge for this kind of dietary variety will strike. You can see the signs of such an attitude easily enough: the animal just lunges at whatever happens to be floating in the water nearby, not even bothering to "check it out" beforehand. If you come across a spider in your cellar or you whack a fly with a shoe and it's not particularly squished, throw it in the tank.

MISCELLANEOUS OTHER FOODS

Once a slider has grown accustomed to captivity and begins trusting you, there won't be much it won't take in the way of foodstuffs. When you have reached this point, start offering items that may not neces-sarily be normal for the species, but will be beneficial nevertheless. For the sake of variety, even bits of lean beef (hamburger meat), ham, turkey, or chicken won't do too much harm. Fruits can be offered along with vegetables, as can pieces of whole-grain breads and cereals. Don't be afraid to experiment. If you think the sliders will benefit from the meal, give it to them, but be sure to avoid things that are too fatty.

Vitamin supplementation is important for all captive slider turtles, but the keeper should remember not to overdo it. This is a tendency suffered by many beginners. Photo of Northern Orbigny's Slider, *Trachemys dorbigni brasiliensis*, by M. Freiberg.

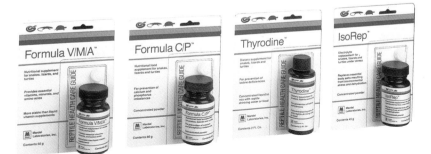

There are many turtle-oriented products being made by Mardel Laboratories, and you don't need to be a veterinarian to know how to use them.

Adult pair of Red-eared Sliders, *Trachemys scripta elegans*. Photo by Isabelle Francais.

VITAMIN SUPPLEMENTS

The final factor in slider turtle feeding lies in vitamin supplementation. Sometimes this type of additive is necessary to assure the animal's health, to make up for what might be lacking elsewhere.

There are a number of products on the market that relate to this, but the best are the ones that are "multi-vitamin" complexes. These can be given either orally or mixed with food, about once every month. There is always the danger of offering too much (hypervitaminosis) which can lead to liver and kidney problems, so usage should be conservative and sparing. Powders work better than liquids when given in conjunction with foodstuffs, but liquids are preferable when given orally.

DR. HERBERT R. AXELROD

Trachemys scripta callirostris (Colombian Slider). Look for signs of undernourishment around the arms and legs. If the skin is limp and scrawny, the turtle might need to eat more.

The Red-eared Slider, *Trachemys scripta elegans.*

DR. HERBERT R. AXELROD

W. P. MARA

The Yellow-bellied Slider, *Trachemys scripta scripta*.

THE FEEDING SCHEDULE

Like all living creatures, *Trachemys* turtles eat on a somewhat organized basis. They are generally active during daylight hours, and thus eat most often during this time.

A keeper should form some sort of routine schedule that is not only sensible for the turtles but practical and convenient for him- or herself. I like to feed my sliders a good-sized meal once every other day. I find this not only fulfills their dietary requirements but also leaves them just hungry enough so that they will not fuss during the next feeding, but instead show great enthusiasm. A finicky reptile is a source of great stress to its keeper, but an eager one will bring great pleasure.

The amount given will depend on the turtle's size. You have to judge for yourself how much the animal should take. A baby turtle will need to eat slightly more often than an adult (since it is in a very sensitive growth stage), but the meals will obviously have to be a lot smaller. Experiment with different amounts, letting your own instincts guide you, and see what the results are. Look for the signs in and around the arms and legs. Does the skin bulge and bloat? Perhaps you have been giving the animal too much. On the other hand, the limbs may seem thin, and the skin scrawny. In that case it may be time to up the portions.

BREEDING

We have come to an age in the herpetological hobby when more and more patrons are beginning to get a better grip on effective techniques for successfully reproducing their own herptiles in captivity. Snakes have probably been the most common products of this advancement, then lizards.

Beyond that, turtles and tortoises place a comfortable third. As with the former two, some species are easier to breed than others. The good news for the slider enthusiast is that virtually all *Trachemys* fall into the former category. They have been bred many times in domestic surroundings, and I might even go so far as to say they are the best turtles to keep if you are a "beginning" breeder.

ARTIFICIAL HIBERNATION

The first step toward successfully breeding a captive slider is successfully hibernating it. And the first step there is correct preparation.

Before anything else, a slider's digestive tract must be emptied out completely. If not, excess foods will ferment and rupture the stomach or intestinal walls, causing death.

A slider can be effectively "flushed"

by first not feeding it at least one week (preferably two) before the actual temperature drop begins, and then, during the final 3 or 4 days, soaking the slider in warm water, which will help the animal defecate.

It should be noted that any turtle which seems malnourished or otherwise emaciated should not be considered a candidate for hibernation at all. Often these animals simply do not have the stored fats necessary to sustain them during times of dormancy, and consequently the "fuel" will simply "run out," killing the host in doing so. A keeper should thus make every effort to be sure his or her slider stock is healthy and well-fed during times of vernal enterprise.

Along similar lines, a keeper may want to consider not hibernating newborns during their first winter, but instead simply keep them warmed and attend to their feeding as usual. Young turtles are often too delicate for the stress of winter torpor and do not survive even in a reasonably controlled situation. It has been suggested that the mortality rate among turtles during their first year is as high as 85 %. Since they will not be "breedable" during their

R. D. BARTLETT

Thanks to the efforts of captive-breeding, striking albino slider specimens like the Red-eared Slider, *Trachemys scripta elegans*, shown here, are now available to the interested hobbyist.

first two years of life, it is suggested that you simply keep them warm and active until their bodies "toughen up" enough to handle the rigors of hibernation.

In any case, once you have properly prepped your turtles, the better for smaller specimens and allow you the freedom of hibernating each specimen individually.

The reason for the mud is obvious—the sliders will burrow into this just as they would in the wild. It is a bit messy however, and may be

W. P. MARA

As fascinating as turtle reproduction seems, every now and then something goes awry. Usually when two turtles are born this way they die within a few months. A joined pair of Red-eared Sliders (*Trachemys scripta elegans*).

next step is to provide the hibernation quarters. This can be done one of two ways.

The first is probably the closer to their natural surroundings but is a little more difficult for the keeper to provide. It involves filling a large container with water then bedding the container with about 6 to 8 inches of mud. The best containers I've used have been large plastic horse troughs (50-gallon sizes seem to work best) since a number of specimens can be hibernated at once. Or if you prefer, a series of plastic sweater boxes can be used. These are troublesome for the hobbyist, but it does give the turtles a strong sense of home, which is important if your pets are wild-caught.

The second technique is a bit more terrestrial and calls for the use of, again, either a large container for multiple occupants or a smaller one for singles or pairs. In this instance you will place a light layer (about an inch or so) of potting soil on the floor of the container, then put in the turtles, and finally cover them with a loose mixture of hay, sphagnum moss, and perhaps a little more soil, until they are totally obscured. This imitates how some turtles will hibernate on land, and although it is a technique generally reserved for box turtles and tortoises, it is also used for some aquatics as well. It is a reasonably carefree method for the average hobbyist and allows closer

must instead fall slowly and carefully over the course of about 2 or 3 days. Since normal active temperature for *Trachemys* turtles is about 80°F, a good hibernation temperature is around 50 to 55°F. That number seems to apply to even the

W. P. MARA

Some keepers have a fascination for oddball freaks like the one shown, but in truth such specimens should really be sacrificed and preserved because their lives will basically be miserable. By doing this, you are actually being humane.

monitoring of the turtles during the hibernation period.

Once you have settled your sliders into their artificial "hibernaculum" you must then provide the correct temperature. Too low and they will freeze to death. Too high and they will linger in and out of a true hibernative state, clicking their metabolism on and off in such a way whereby fats will be burned at a greater pace and the animal will not survive a full resting term. Furthermore, the temperature drop that places them into dormancy cannot be abrupt but

southernmost species, but any lower than that is getting risky. The reason the temperature must not be dropped too quickly is because even the hardiest turtle's body cannot take that kind of shock. There is a better than average chance such a thing will kill them.

There are a number of ways to provide the proper hibernation temperature, but if you live in a tropical or even subtropical zone, this could mean expense. For those keepers like myself who live in temperate regions, furnishing winter temperatures is easy—simply hibernate the turtles in the winter. Place your sliders in a room that is not normally affected by household heat during the proper season. A cellar is a good place, as is an attic. If the room you have chosen is not champagne is perfect), although they will be somewhat expensive. The advantage, however, to such a thing is that you can hypothetically hibernate your stock any time you wish.

W. P. MARA

Plastron of "pastel" Red-eared Slider, *Trachemys scripta elegans*. The specimen shown is an immature female.

quite cold enough, open a window a little bit. If you are afraid the room may get too cold, you can always purchase a small heater with an internal thermostat. I have used these with much success in the past and highly advise them.

On the other hand, if you live in an area where the ambient temperature does not drop to the appropriate level, you may have to consider purchasing some sort of refrigeration unit (the type that restaurants use for

CONSIDERATIONS AFTER HIBERNATION

Just as you would not abruptly drop a slider's temperature in order to spark hibernation, neither should you take them out of it too quickly. Do not remove them from their winter containers, but instead warm up the room itself. If for some reason this is not possible, remove the containers entirely and place them in a more appropriate chamber (keeping in mind that a large tub filled with water will be extremely heavy).

Let the temperature rise over a day or two then remove the animals by hand and return them to their normal quarters. They will probably need another day or two in order to re-orient themselves, so do not

MATING TIME

About 2 weeks after hibernation has ended and your sliders have been properly fed, it is time to breed them. The keeper must first provide an adequate site for this to occur in. It is important to note that until you are

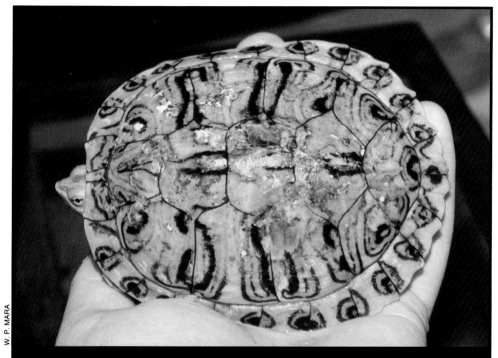

Another product of selective breeding is the "pastel" variety of the Red-eared Slider, *Trachemys scripta elegans*. This beautiful variant is now being bred regularly, although the offspring still command a respectable price.

attempt to feed them until about the fourth or fifth day. When they do start feeding, be sure to give them a little more than they are used to getting to compensate for what they lost during the winter. The idea is to get them back to peak health and weight as quickly as possible so the breeding process will go smoothly. Unhealthy males will have a lack of interest in mating and unhealthy females will not produce fertile eggs or may not be able to withstand the strain of pregnancy.

ready to breed your sliders, the males and females should be kept apart.

The breeding tank need not be overly large, although again, the larger the better. The aforementioned heavy plastic horse trough is a wonderful choice, as are children's wading pools. If neither of these are available to you, a 20-gallon aquarium (per pair) will do.

The water in the tank need only be about 5 inches deep and reasonably warm. Do not add any rocks or other obstacles, as these things will not

JIM MERLI

The albino variation of the Red-eared Slider, *Trachemys scripta elegans*, is probably the only albino turtle of any kind that appears with regularity in the pet market.

help. Place the two turtles in at the same time and then wait. It is advised that you keep a safe distance from the pair since turtles are more easily distracted than most other herps; about 10 to 15 feet away is appropriate. From there you should be able to observe what's happening and stand by in case of any problems.

If everything proceeds normally, the male will start by swimming toward the female and try to caress her face with his elongated front

male completion of his "courtship ritual" and then he will move behind and mount her, entwining their tails so the two vents meet and copulation can take place. The male's plastron is concave so the entire process is made easier for him. Since there is no need for the females to possess such a modification, their plastrons are flat—a dead giveaway for telling the sexes apart in adult specimens (something much more difficult to do with the young).

The entire mating procedure takes

It is important to remember that newborn slider turtles need a basking spot more so than the adults do. If they are not provided with one, most, if not all, will drown. Photo of Orbigny's Slider, *Trachemys dorbigni*.

claws. He may also swim around her in circles. If she is receptive she will not resist further advances, but sometimes this will not be the case and a mild fight may break out. If you witness this taking place, or if nothing occurs at all within the first 30 to 45 minutes, remove the pair to their repsective quarters and try them again in a day or two.

If on the other hand your luck is good and your sliders do as they are expected, the female will permit the

place in a fairly short time—about 10 to 15 minutes—and afterward it is advised that you remove the pair and return them to their separate tanks. If you would like, you can try mating them again over the next 2 weeks, but beyond that time the female will be well into her pregnancy and should not be disturbed too much.

CARE OF THE FEMALES DURING THE GESTATION PERIOD

As with any other living creature, a

Only the healthiest adult sliders, like the beautiful Red-eared Slider, *Trachemys scripta elegans*, specimen shown here, should be used for breeding purposes. Photo by Isabelle Francais.

pregnant slider must be treated with the utmost prudence. Since the eggs are being fertilized and developed during this time, any violent movements can seriously hinder that process. The mothers should be handled only when absolutely necessary.

You can make their gestation period a little easier by giving sharper attention to the husbandry basics.

concerned with the sudden change as it is quite normal. Of course, a keeper will still want to offer food on a regular basis; often the females will simply eat less but not stop altogether. Also consider the possibility of a temporary change in dietary preference. Often I have seen pregnant *Trachemys* regress into being worm, cricket, and vegetable eaters and toss commercial food to

Every now and then, a bizarre pattern turns up in captive-bred stock. The belly pattern of this Red-eared Slider, *Trachemys scripta elegans*, for example, is a bit different from the norm.

Clean water is always a requirement, but double your efforts to assure it during this time. Also be sure the mothers are not too cramped in their tanks; if you feel you have too many in one aquarium then buy another. Correct heating is also very important, as is the faithful provision of full-spectrum lighting since they will probably spend a lot of time basking. In the wild they do this in order to warm their bodies, thus warming the eggs at the same time.

One habit that pregnant sliders may display during this time, and which alarms many keepers, is a stubborn refusal to eat. Do not be

the wind. Before you have decided your pregnant slider has given up food for the duration, try a number of things.

EGGLAYING TIME

The average gestation period for an adult female slider is about 2 months in the wild, although if they cannot find a suitable nesting site they will retain their eggs, thus invalidating such a time estimation. Toward the last week or two, the females will begin displaying their natural nesting behavior. In captivity this usually manifests itself in the mother turtle spending abnormally long periods of time on land, scratching, sniffing, and digging around for potential egglaying sites. She will do this on whatever land mass you happen to provide, and if it is an area that contains a soft substrate like potting day. The average number of eggs in a slider's clutch can be anywhere from two to 20.

INCUBATION/CARE OF THE EGGS

When a mother slider is given

There is not one, but a handful of "pastel" Red-eared Slider, *Trachemys scripta elegans*, varieties, the one shown here being one of the most breathtaking.

soil or similar, she may begin to dig a few "test nests."

This is the time when you should carefully remove the mother and place her in her nesting quarters, set up specifically for egglaying. This need not be any larger than a 20-gallon tank, but rather than mostly water it should be filled with about 4 inches of potting soil or a potting soil/vermiculite mixture. Watch the mother as often as you can so you know when and where her eggs have been laid. If you cannot afford the time to monitor her that closely, at least check around the tank once a proper egglaying facilities, she will, in essence, dig a hole, drop her clutch, and leave. In captivity it is then the responsibility of the keeper to see that they are incubated properly.

Some keepers I have spoken with prefer to bed the nesting box with the accepted vermiculite, etc., then allow the mother to lay as she would normally, and simply leave the eggs where they are rather than remove and replace them in a separate incubation container. This option has its good and bad points.

For one, it is never a good idea to handle reptile eggs except in times of necessity. Since a mother lays hers in an obscured pile, digging down to find them can be a risky business. By leaving the eggs in the nesting box you more or less avoid this completely.

However, monitoring buried eggs can be somewhat difficult. The only thing a keeper can do is lightly dig through the substrate and hope he or she doesn't put a finger through one in the process. A worst-case scenario

finally hatch, some of them may have trouble working their way to the surface and may even suffocate. You would conceivably then have to check the nest at least once a day to prevent this catastrophe.

Thus I will take a stand and say the second option—removing the eggs from the mother's nest and placing them in their own container—is infinitely superior to the former. Granted, the

R. D. BARTLETT

Apparently, natural intergradation is fairly common with the slider turtles (in the correct localities, that is), and thus it can be assumed that it is also possible with captive stock as well. Shown is a cross between the Red-eared Slider, *Trachemys scripta elegans*, and the Yellow-bellied Slider, *Trachemys scripta scripta*.

here involves one of the eggs going bad, and instead of being removed (because the hobbyist cannot see it), the ensuing rot and fungal growth spread and infect some of the healthy eggs as well.

Furthermore, when the young

task of locating the eggs and then removing them without harm is a dicey affair, but the freedoms beyond that are a luxury to the enthusiast.

The incubation box need not be elaborate. The trend in herpetology today is to use a large plastic sweater box or, in the case of a smaller clutch, a plastic shoebox. I must agree with this and say from experience that these serve their purpose extremely well. They can be obtained in many places (supermarkets, department stores, home improvement centers, etc.) and are not expensive. The nice thing about plastic is that it is both easy to work with (it can be cleaned to allow for ventilation. The holes should not be too wide in diameter (no more than a quarter of an inch) or number beyond about a dozen. If there are too many holes or they are too large, moisture will quickly escape and the eggs will dry out.

Bed the container with about a 2-inch layer of vermiculite. It should be of heavy grain rather than fine, as I

The Red-eared Slider, *Trachemys scripta elegans*, is not the only subspecies with a "red ear." Shown here is the Venezuelan Slider, *Trachemys scripta chichiriviche*.

the point of near sterility) and is durable enough to be re-used for years and years. It also responds appropriately to moisture, which is of course a crucial consideration when incubating reptile eggs.

Once the keeper has obtained the incubation container, a series of small holes should be drilled into the lid to have found the former to produce much better results (although I can't honestly say I know why). Vermiculite can be purchased at any store that sells garden supplies. It is used extensively in the horticultural field as a moisture retentant, and is thus used for the same purpose here.

Moisten the vermiculite by running

a light trickle of warm water down one wall of the container while churning the bedding with your free hand. The idea is to make the vermiculite damp, not wet. If it has the gloppy consistency of oatmeal then you've overdone it; throw about half of it out and add some fresh material.

Moving the eggs into the container can be nerve-wracking, and if you don't honestly think you have a steady enough hand, then find someone who does. The procedure involves slowly and carefully scooping back small sections of the substrate around the nest, feeling all the time with your fingertips for the eggs. Once you uncover one, before you do anything else, take a water-based felt-tipped marker and make a small mark on the top of the shell. The reason for this is obvious—you will always know where the top is. Then, place each egg carefully in the incubation chamber, set the container somewhere where it will not be disturbed, and simply check the eggs every few days (by lifting the lid, but not moving the eggs about), keeping an eye out for eggs that have gone bad (which should be thrown out immediately) or any developing fungal growth (which can be removed by lightly wiping the eggs with a soft

MICHAEL GILROY

In the wild, the mortality rate for newborn sliders is frighteningly high. Many never even hatch because the egg nests are raided by hungry predators.

paintbrush dipped in a 50/50 mixture of antiseptic mouthwash and water).

HATCHING/CARE OF YOUNG

About 80 to 85 days after the eggs have been laid, a keeper should begin watching them closely because hatching time is drawing near. When the big day arrives, the tiny turtles, which will not measure over an inch and a half, will cut through their shells by way of something called the *egg tooth*, which will fall off about an hour later and never regenerate. The neonates will then remain in their shells for another day or perhaps even longer if they do not feel secure enough. Do not attempt to pick them up until they have done so. When you finally do, you may notice a small sac on their plastrons. This is known as the yolk sac and was responsible for providing the baby slider with nutrition during embryonic development. It is extremely important that the keeper does not remove this—the turtle will absorb the rest of the contents in a very short time and the sac will fall off on its own. If you try to remove it yourself you will very probably kill the animal, so just let it be. After it finally drops off you will notice a "split" in the plastron. This too will heal over the course of time and should not be treated by the keeper.

Now that the clutch has hatched out and a new brood of sliders has been born, the first thing the keeper needs to do is set them up in their new home and get them feeding. Since young sliders are so small, a 20-gallon tank per dozen will be more than adequate. Be absolutely sure you provide the young sliders with a dry land area that they can access easily. Many people do not realize that a newborn aquatic turtle is actually prone to drowning and many have done so due to

and that coupled with the fact that they are captive-bred should make feeding them quite easy.

It doesn't matter so much which item they choose to favor, as long as they eat *something*. The first 4 or 5 years of a slider's life are the most essential in terms of growth and development, so proper nutrition is a major priority. Running down the list of known slider items one by one is a sensible approach. Start with the items that are the easiest for you to supply. Unlike many adult sliders

A simple incubation box can be made by placing a layer of heavily granular vermiculite and some sphagnum moss into a plastic shoebox. The vermiculite and the moss are then moistened and the lid (with a few tiny holes drilled through it) is put on top. Photo by W. P. Mara.

negligence on the part of the keeper. Unlike the adults, young turtles do not have the ability to stay underwater for excessively long periods of time. Furthermore, their tiny legs tire out rather quickly and most neonates will not master the floating technique right out of the shell. A simple brick or two laid in a shallow water body will serve the purpose, as will a number of other things.

The next step is to get them feeding. Fortunately, sliders have, as I mentioned already, a fairly varied diet,

(particularly wild-caughts, who are already set in their ways), captive newborns seem to respond well to commercial turtle food. Since this is easy to acquire through pet stores or mail order, I suggest you try it first. Remember to break the pieces into bits small enough to fit into their tiny mouths. This of course applies to any other foods as well.

As with any captive adult turtle, newborns should be exposed to full-spectrum lighting as soon as possible. This is especially important with neonates since their shells are very soft at birth and will need the D3 in order to harden. A full-spectrum photoperiod of 6 hours per day with

remainder of their lives (unless of course the goal is to begin a breeding colony from scratch).

There are a number of avenues one

WILLIAM B. ALLEN, JR.

If you look closely you will be able to see the egg tooth on the very new Red-eared Slider, *Trachemys scripta elegans*. This tooth will fall off a few hours later and never grow back. It is there purely to assist the neonate with its task of cutting through the shell.

normal light filling out the rest of the time is suggested. With normal growth, a slider turtle should reach sexual maturity in five or six years.

Finally, a question of what to do with a hoard of newborn turtles after you have "gotten them going" presents itself, as most keepers do not wish to have a dozen or so around for the

can choose from. First, there is the noble idea of replenishing wild populations by releasing some of your "extras." The problems with this is that often a captive-bred animal will "pick up" certain germs that may not only be harmful to them, but will then pass on to the wild colonies they have been introduced into. In the worst-case

K. AND D. ZINCK

The act of painting images on turtle shells is not only cruel and idiotic, but it also prevents the turtles from receiving the direct sunlight they need to survive.

scenario the colonies in question could conceivably be wiped out completely as a result of the right type of disease. As unlikely as this may sound, it has been known to happen.

Furthermore, many turtles will adapt to captivity so quickly that their natural instincts will be stunted in development and thus placing them in the wild would be cruel. On the same line, if a young slider has already grown accustomed to commercial food, it's certainly not going to find much of it in a quiet woodland pond somewhere.

Thus a second option is to simply sell your excess young. Needless to say, many herpetologists do this, some to the point where captive breeding reptiles and amphibians can now be looked upon as a legitimate business. The procedure for becoming involved in this aspect of the hobby seems simple enough: place an ad in any of the popular herpetological magazines or society newsletters and either advertise what you have or invite the reader to send for a price list. There doesn't seem to be much more to it than that. Keep in mind though that

this can lead to some interaction with the postal system, and since turtles can only be legally shipped air freight, many hassles may soon follow. Other than that, you can rent a table at a local herp swap meet and sidestep the mail order business altogether. Keep in mind that there is a law in the United States forbidding the sale of *any* turtle with a shell length of under four inches.

Which bears into the final option—simply trading your sliders for other turtles rather than selling them outright. I am both surprised and disappointed that the trading of herptiles does not occur more often. It is dangerous to continually promote the hobby of herpetology from a commercial perspective. It gives outsiders the impression that keeping herps is more business than hobby, and that is not good. If you take the time to work out trades with others like yourself, you will find your own herp collection will grow and allow you to then maintain and propagate other reptiles and amphibians that you otherwise might never have the opportunity to keep.

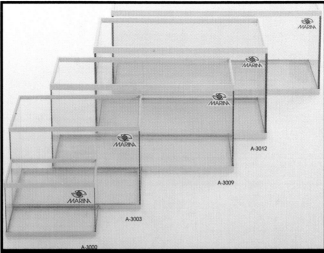

A-3012

A-3009

A-3003

A-3000

Aquarium tanks used to house sliders and other semi-aquatic and aquatic turtles are available at pet shops not only in different sizes but also in different configurations, with some being more square in shape and others more elongated, as shown in this array of Marina Aquariums.

The eyes are an important indicator of health in captive red-eared sliders. This bright-eyed specimen is healthy.

There are a remarkable number of diseases that can attack a captive slider, and you as a responsible keeper should be made aware of at least most of the common ones. Turtles, unlike other herptiles, have an amazing constitution and will probably not reveal signs of an illness until the conditions have already developed beyond safe stages. Thus, it is up to the hobbyist to identify and act upon any and all disease symptoms before the promise of fatality occurs.

DISEASES

Salmonella

Probably the one disease most often associated with turtles, the concern and "panic" for salmonella has, fortunately, begun to recede over the last few years. Before that time, however, it was a major issue in connection with keeping turtles as pets that eventually led to the 1975 Food and Drug Administration's ban on the sale of turtles with a carapace length of under 4 inches.

Salmonellosis is an intestinal infection that attacks many living organisms, humans among them, and is brought on by bacteria belonging to the group *Salmonella*. There are many hundreds of bacteria types contained within this classification and many animals besides turtles are known carriers. Salmonella is most commonly transmitted from chelonians via filthy surroundings, i.e., dirty water, feces that have been ignored rather than removed, etc. The turtles themselves contract the bacteria from infected food sources given during shipping, or from close contact with other infected turtles while sitting in giant vats of water in a distributor's warehouse waiting to be moved on to a pet store. It goes without saying that salmonellosis is highly contagious.

The way the disease is passed on to a human is obvious: a keeper comes in contact with an infected turtle, thus infecting his or her own

All imported slider specimens, like the Hispaniolan Slider, *Trachemys decorata*, shown here, should be suspected of illness and quarantined before being put with your other stock.

DR. PETER C. H. PRITCHARD

self, and then fails to take proper sanitary measures afterward, i.e., thoroughly washing the hands and arms, etc. Children are probably the

regardless of its age and size. The problem lies not so much in the animal but in the amount of attention a keeper gives to the cleanliness of

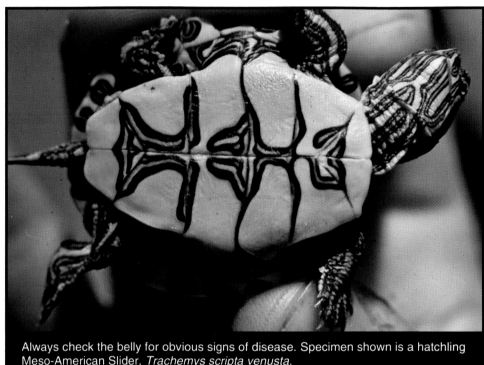

Always check the belly for obvious signs of disease. Specimen shown is a hatchling Meso-American Slider, *Trachemys scripta venusta*.

most perpetual victims, which is why the sale of tiny turtles was outlawed in the first place—kids would stick their pet turtle in their mouths. The sliders, the Red-eared, *Trachemys scripta elegans*, in particular, caught most of the heat for bringing salmonella to these youngsters, and by the early 70's over a quarter of a million cases had been documented although whether or not most of these cases were directly related to baby turtles is unknown.

The sad fact is, salmonellosis still exists today, and probably always will. Although the laws and regulations inspired by it have helped to some degree, a keeper can still contract it from a captive slider

his or her captives.

And therein lies the "cure" if you will. A slider that has been infected by salmonella to the point whereby the keeper can easily identify the symptoms (these are faint at best—no appetite, general lethargy, sometimes diarrhea) can and should only be attended to by a veterinarian, and quickly at that because once it reaches this stage the animal is usually dead within a week. Again, the idea is to avoid it in the first place through proper sanitary measures. A slider's water must be changed frequently whether it is filtered or not, and the tank must be scrubbed well during the interim. Furthermore, a keeper must wash his or her own self very thoroughly since the threat of becoming infected is nothing to be taken lightly. The only true way to battle salmonellosis is to avoid it in the first place.

Sore or Swollen Eyes

Often a slider will show signs of a mild ocular infection that will attack the eye itself, becoming quite swollen and boasting an alarming "bulging" appearance. Sometimes the turtle will show this problem as it sits in the pet store tank, then on the other hand a keeper will not encounter it until well after the animal has been purchased and spent time in its new home.

Unless the condition is severe, the hobbyist should not be alarmed. Swollen eyes are a common problem among aquatic turtles and can be remedied easily enough. The reason a slider will develop the condition in the first place (90 % of the time) has to do with the keeper failing to keep the animal's water clean. Since sliders spend so much of their time submerged, the bacteria in the filthy water will most violently attack the eyes and cause them to swell.

The condition can be treated by

E. ELKAN

Swollen eyes are a common problem with aquatic turtles of all kinds. The illness usually arises (literally) when the turtles are forced to live in filthy water. An infected Red-eared Slider, *Trachemys scripta elegans*.

swabbing the eyes with a cotton swab coated with diluted boric acid (60/40 %) or the old standard sulfamethiazine. The keeper must also change the water at once, cleaning the tank throughly in the process and then faithfully continuing to do so from then on. Recovery is usually rapid, but if the problem persists then a vet should be called on. Otherwise, complications could occur, and permanent blindness is indeed a possibility.

Softening of the Shell

Possibly the most common problem suffered by captive turtles, softening of the shell can and often does lead to death.

It is caused by a lack of calcium and is easily noticed through the obvious symptoms, although it can be a bit harder to detect in very young specimens since their shells will be somewhat soft to begin with (in their case the shells sometimes turn bleach white, in patches).

The reason soft shell arises in captivity can almost always be found in the husbandry. Most captive sliders receive full-spectrum lighting and get calcium through a varied diet. The latter is a good example as to why mealworms cannot completely make up this diet—they do not provide sufficient calcium. Furthermore, soft shell is the first disorder your slider will develop if not given full-spectrum lighting.

with a tiny wad of jelly (any flavor) it will adhere to the food item a lot better. Remember that sliders are aquatic, so sprinkling a mealworm,

Perhaps the most devastating captive-induced disease is soft shell, most often caused by the keeper who fails to provide his or her pets with full-spectrum lighting. Photo of a diseased neonatal Red-eared Slider, *Trachemys scripta elegans*.

You can avoid this problem, or in its earlier stage cure it, by simply increasing your turtle's full-spectrum light hours, or, if you have not purchased this type of bulb yet, then do so immediately. Furthermore, altering the animal's diet to include more calcium-rich meals is very helpful, but if you feel you cannot do this with sufficient effectiveness, then buy calcium powder from your local pet store and simply empty the contents onto a food item, doing this about once a month. I have found that if you mix the "calcium powder"

etc., with a powder may prove useless since the powder will simply disperse the moment it hits the water. Since sliders are such eager, voracious feeders, I find I achieve the best results by: 1) mixing some calcium powder with a small wad of jelly; 2) spreading the jelly on a cricket, mealworm, small piece of meat, etc.; and then 3) dangling the item just above the water so the turtle has to reach up for it. If your sliders are comfortable enough with your presence and with their captive home, they should respond to this "hand-feeding" technique without a problem. The reason for this of course is to get the enriched food into their mouth before it has the chance to liquefy.

the cold, but moisture certainly affects the body in many negative ways, especially when in combination with other agents.

For example, a slider turtle kept in a room that is prone to drafts will

When soft shell advances to the stage shown here, chances are the turtle will not survive.

W. P. MARA

Respiratory Infections

There are a multitude of respiratory infections that attack captive reptiles and amphibians, and although most of them are mild and can be treated with success during the early stages, the few that remain can be vicious and take a life with amazing speed.

Slider turtles, along with other aquatic species, are particularly susceptible to such problems, and the fact that they spend most of their time in the water definitely plays a part. We as humans can relate to this easily enough by recalling our parents's warnings about catching cold in the rain. Doctors will tell you that the rain itself does not "cause"

develop some sort of respiratory infection just as you or I would. This is one of the more common causes of such an ailment, and probably so because of its subtlety. You would of course never keep a captive slider in a room that felt like a wind tunnel, but obvious drafts are not usually the problem. It only takes a few cold breezes to set off an infection of this sort. Keeping a room tightly sealed is of utmost importance.

Also, the majority of respiratory infections are contagious, so quarantining your new animals is advised. The symptoms to watch for include runny noses, a turtle that does not keep its mouth fully closed (or wheezes), and in many cases an infected aquatic turtle will swim lopsided, the ailing lung being the one on the lower side. Other obvious signs such as lethargy and a refusal to eat will be present as well.

If you think you have identified the

antibiotic drug which you will have to administer yourself.

Fungus/Fungal Infections

Occasionally you may see what looks like a light layer of cotton on

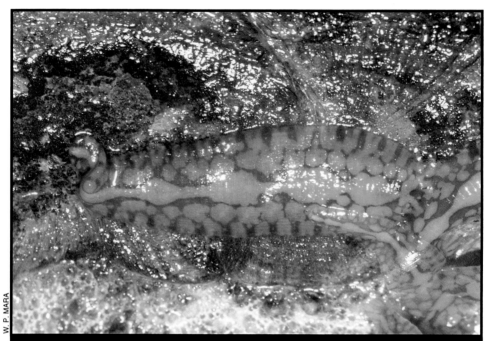

Always check new specimens for signs of leeches. Leeches are commonly found on aquatic turtles. They can be removed by being stretched from the turtle's body with a pair of tweezers, then submitted to the flame of a cigarette lighter.

problem in its early stages, the road to eradicating it may be a simple one. Again, make every effort to keep drafts out, and check to make sure the temperature is set at an appropriate level. Warmth is perhaps the most crucial provision when treating this disease in the home. Also, the sick slider should be removed from its quarters and placed alone in a new, clean tank. Make sure the water is warm as well.

If after a week the condition persists or worsens, bring the turtle to a veterinarian. He or she may either be able to treat the patient right there, or at least prescribe an

your slider's shell. This problem is more common with aquatic turtles, particularly the young. Chances are it is some form of fungus, and although somewhat alarming in appearance, can usually be treated with full expectations of recovery unless of course for some reason it has been allowed to spread across most of the body, in which case the animal should be handed over to a vet.

In the hobbyist's home, you can treat the problem by immersing the slider in a salt water bath (remember to keep the water warm) for about a half an hour each day. Furthermore, you can actually give your turtles a "bath" in the same solution and utilize a soft sponge, gently scrubbing the infected regions. This method may speed recovery slightly. As long as the problem is not severe, you should witness the first stages of

and/or constipation may be the problem you're dealing with.

The reason for these problems can usually be found in the diet. Perhaps the most important element to a turtle's diet is variety, so giving it the

All aquatic turtles can fall victim to shell fungus and should be checked regularly for it. The shells should be as clean as that on this Cumberland Slider, *Trachemys scripta troosti.*

recovery within a day or two, and full recovery in about 10 days to 2 weeks.

Intestinal Infections (Diarrhea and Constipation, Blockage, etc.)

Sometimes a slider turtle will have trouble with its intestinal tract, and this can manifest itself in a number of ways. Blockage of the gut is one of the more common examples, and can cause further infections which could very easily kill your pet. A keeper can notice this problem when he or she realizes foods have been going into an animal and little or nothing has been coming out.

Along similar lines, a turtle's feces should not be runny or off-colored, and if this is the case then diarrhea

same food every day, day after day, will usually result in some kind of intestinal upset. This is particularly common with turtles that are given commercial foods; the keeper feels the canned product provides the animal with enough vitamins, etc., to keep it healthy and happy, and does not want to bother supplying anything else. While the nutrient makeup of these products may be reliable, the simple fact that they cannot provide variety makes them partial at best.

A cure is simple enough, provided of course the problem has not gotten completely out of hand (you may want to take a stool sample to a vet to be sure this is the case). Give the

Perhaps the best way to provide any slider turtle with full-spectrum lighting is to leave it in an outdoor enclosure and let the sun do it for you. Photo of an adult Red-eared Slider, *Trachemys scripta elegans*, by R. T. Zappalorti.

SALLY ANNE THOMPSON

Newborn slider turtles are in greater need of full-spectrum lighting than adults are, for they will need all they can get during their first few years of growth.

Note how dry the shell of this Venezuelan Slider, *Trachemys scripta chichiriviche*, looks. A keeper must remember that although slider turtles love to bask, they are still aquatic and need to spend much of their time in water.

R. D. BARTLETT

The head of a beautiful albino adult male red-eared slider, *Trachemys scripta elegans*.

DR. PETER C. H. PRITCHARD

When a slider turtle has been forced to travel due to importation, you can almost guarantee it will be suffering from some kind of disease or another. The time from when the animal is packed until it is placed in its new home can often be weeks or even months. Specimen shown is a Huastecan Slider, *Trachemys scripta cataspila.*

slider a bath in separate tank of warm water at 5-hour periods every day until the gut is "flushed out." Then start the animal on some new foods. Rarely will you encounter a slider that will take one item and one item only, so this should not be a problem. You may have to go out of your way to obtain certain things, but that just goes with the territory. Starchy items are not particularly good for a slider's system, but in small quantities they will help tighten things up and get the animal "normal" again. Once recovery has been assured, design a new, more varied diet for the turtle and stick to it responsibly.